"Truth is Justice's drunken sister./ She jaywalks, spits on the sidewalk,/ burns books in the courtyard,/ pulls tongues from the root." And the truth we get in Craig Paulenich's *Old Brown* is no easy truth. Powerful and unwavering, Paulenich digs deep into nineteenth century history, using Captain John Brown as a touchstone to illuminate America's uneasy relationship with race and its obsession with violence. Part poetry, part history, Paulenich's portrait is an indictment of our contemporary times, his John Brown both prophet and terrorist, hero and cold-blooded killer, an everyman for our schizophrenic America. In stunningly imaginative poems that range from catalogs of the dead to lyric meditations on religion's role in our complicity, Paulenich masterfully connects the dots from Harper's Ferry to our modern terrorist state, pointing out along the way that "Slavery is the American Leviathan, and we,/ Jonah's all, rattle about inside its brass ribs."

—Peter Grandbois, author of *Kissing the Lobster*

OTHER BOOKS BY CRAIG PAULENICH

Drift of the Hunt (Nobodaddies Press, 2006)
Blood Will Tell (BlazeVOX [books], 2009)

Beneath a Single Moon: Buddhism and Contemporary American Poetry
(Editor, with Kent Johnson, Shambhala Press, 1991)

BOTTOM DOG PRESS

HURON, OHIO

OLD BROWN

CRAIG PAULENICH

APPALACHIAN SERIES
BOTTOM DOG PRESS
HURON, OHIO

ISBN: 978-1-947504-11-0
Bottom Dog Press, Inc.
PO Box 425, Huron, OH 44839
Lsmithdog@aol.com
http://smithdocs.net

CREDITS:
General Editor: Larry Smith
Cover & Layout Design: Susanna Sharp-Schwacke
Author Photo: Lit Youngstown

Special Thanks to the Kansas Historical Society
for the use of the John Brown photo on page 87.

Table of Contents

I would remind you that extremism in the defense of liberty is no vice.
~Old Brown

—You know father. He will dally till he is trapped.

The Shenandoah and Potomac
bring their hands together in prayer,
Harpers Ferry the press plate
between their palms.

I

LET THERE BE A GOD

Let there be a God in his secret honey-hole,
a God big as Barnum, slippery as the Feejee Mermaid,
one who smells a donut frying five miles away.

Let there be a Milky Way above and an Underground Railroad below.

Let there be a God with a mind like an octopus,
God like a mouthful of teeth, like a stropped razor,
a God of tea not coffee, a God without butter.
Let there be a lantern in the house above the river.

Let there be a God of shearing and lambing,
the dead rising in cairns, the dead
reminding us of the dead to come,
a God who reads the placenta for rips and tears,
who returns the prolapsed uterus to the spent body,
a God who keeps the weasel out of the moonlit coop,
the fox from the barn swollen with hay,
who bottles lightning in glass globes staked
along the barn roof's ridgelines.

Let there be a God like Drano.
A God whose bales of wool are weighted with wattle.

He parts the Ohio at Marietta,
trips the traps, opens the irons.
He is covered in the scars of righteousness.
He takes his silence on the Sabbath.
He heals the grub-worm.
Let there be a lantern in the house above the river.

May he confound the slave-catcher,
soul reduced to pieces of silver.
May he be a God like grapeshot,
who leads with columns of smoke and fire.
May God's pea-sized heart be hard enough for the elect
to feel beneath their many mattresses, a willing God
to carpet-bomb a generation of hearts and minds.

Let him be the God of two tablets.
Let him walk his flock through the dip.
Let him keep his own counsel.
And let there always be a lantern in the house above the river.

Love Me, Kill My Enemies

Prove that you love me
And slay my enemies.
Let pigs root in them.
Let them enter Hell
Carrying their eyes
In little pails.
Let their children's children
Eat bitter bread and dandelions
All their days.

OLD BROWN

Old Brown belonged to the Church of the Holy Rifles,
carried a Beecher Bible, sold Fuller Brushes & Chicago Typewriters.
He strangled a copperhead in his crib,
had a blue ox, rolled snakes downhill.
Old Brown slew ten thousand Butternuts with the jawbone of an ass.
Old Brown could smell a donut from five miles away.
He was called The Old Man, Captain Brown, Uncle Charley.
He was Nelson Hawkins and Shubel Morgan.
Old Brown said, *I am the flenser of a vengeful God,*
lay the dead horse of Slavery before me.
Old Brown walked fugitives across Missouri,
then ate dinner with Emerson and Thoreau.
He was the Shilo, a Divine Wind.
He lit a prairie fire that burned down Blanket Hill.
Chaffed and itched, nettled by hypnotism,
he read head bumps like psychic street maps
and waited for the bees to hive.

Old Brown said, *Send lawyers, guns and money.*
He was the Tank of God, the Holy Roller, a souped-up,
street-legal Camaro, a train wreck waiting to happen.
He was Wonderbread and Red Ball Jets,
hated Masons and paper money.
Old Brown was the first to say, *Kill 'em all, God knows His own.*
Old Brown was a big chunk of meat falling through the ceiling.
Old Brown had four thousand sheep, knew each by name,
urged them through the dip like Moses coaxing the Israelites.
His staff wriggled like a serpent.
Old Brown said, *It is the worst possible policy for a man to reveal*
his plans. Old Brown waited.
He thought the bees would hive.

Old Brown said, *Those men had a perfect right to be hung,*
and *All Cretans are liars.*
He was a Know Nothing and a know-it-all,
a Captain in the way that Sanders was a Colonel,
or Bean a Judge. His plans
were sketchy as a Feejee Mermaid.

He would take the war to Africa.
He would rest in God's bower.
Old Brown put the roar in the Roaring Twenties,
the gilt in the Gilded Age, the fun in funeral.
His was the last Good Death.
Old Brown said, *No man sent me.*
Old Brown said, *Eternity behind, eternity before,*
and we the little speck in the center.
Captain Brown was radiant in the coffin.
He was P.T. Barnum with a handgun,
undercard to the main bout,
icy tail of the comet, fable without a moral.
He had a whiff of brimstone about him,
the white eyes of horseless carriages.
He was a sheep of the blackest dye.
There was a broadsword in his dune buggy,
hobgoblins in his meadow.
He wanted the pickaninnies to go Mau Mau,
wanted the black bees to hive.

Old Brown said, *I know no more grammar than a cow.*
Old Brown was God's millstone, cog in Ezekial's wheel,
a U-Haul packed with ammonium nitrate.
He blew the legs off The Thinker and left behind a silver bullet,
bombed the cops in Haymarket Square.
He was cherry blossom, earth-shaker, game-changer, deal-breaker.
He was a gun deck awash in body parts.
He was called The Abominable No Man and No-Name Maddox.
He never let the truth stand in the way of a good story.
Old Brown stood still as a post before a column of tanks,
then danced a two-step with the grinding lead.
He flamed like a saffron monk. He locked arms
with John Lewis and crossed the Edmund Pettis Bridge.
Calvinist Fatalist, Conspiracy Theorist, Liberation Theologist,
Old Brown said, *That will happen, will happen,*
wrote scripture in blood on the livingroom wall,
stashed arms in Ashtabula. Old Brown was
Manson in broadcloth, broadsword to the brainpan,
a Bolshevik who beat the podium with his shoe.
He was Blood Hound and Fateful Lightning,
Murrah's sheared face, bullet through the
back door, Death in the driveway shrubbery.
He was obsessively compulsive, compulsively obsessive.

He said, *No sense, makes sense.*
Old Brown was Ahab without literary merit,
a suicide bomber in frock coat and straw hat.
He belonged to the Divine Thunder God Corps.
He could wait an eternity for the bees to hive.

Old Brown said, *Ask about our automated courtesy rifles.*
Old Brown was a column of fire two hundred feet high,
shape-shifter with ten thousand faces, fourth Magi, third convict.
He was a tenth degree Thugee.
He was the horizon of the sun.
He purged this land with blood.
He said, *I knew they were coming before they knew they were coming.*
Old Brown wasn't interested in hearts and minds.
He was the blind eye of justice, St. Michael's scales,
the shepherd I shall not want.
He dug up his dead each time he moved.
Old Brown had his finger on the button, he was
mutually assured destruction, he was radioactive.
Old Brown was the rain that drowns,
he was the last Puritan.
A coffin pine grew in his yard.
Call him Darryl Bridges or Tim Tuttle,
Sputnik or Clever Odysseus, he is
still moldering in the grave, still
waiting for the bees to hive.

The Subterranean Passageway

—I never went off track and I never lost a passenger.

Runaways dropped down the rabbit hole,
pole star for a pocket watch.
Conjurors, cow-catchers, deranged with drapetomania,
they were mad for Libertyville.
On benches narrow as church pews
they sat down and hung on.

They rode upon iron horses with hooves that sparked,
horses with fetlocks of flame, horses that
spit hot coals and snorted midnight smoke.

Snake heads curled from the tired iron,
dead men were poured into knuckles and bolsters,
sideframes beaten to ploughshares.
Lincoln pins rattled between rolling stock,
the boxcars' deadweight to payload one-to-one.

God's hand was on the throttle
and the ground belched smoke like a prophet.
The Underground Railroad was all function, no form,
stupefying click-clack across cross-ties, sills, sleepers,
call them what you will, until there was no there there.

These were the days when time was willy-nilly,
before they tabled time, drew butcher's lines
across the nation as though she was a cow,
when everything was new, crude and doubtful,
and they followed The Drinking Gourd.

There were Reefers and Pullman Sleepers,
there were Track-Walkers looking for fires.
Where rail lines crossed, the high-ball signaled
all clear, and lawn-jockeys' lanterns
were code for safe houses.

EACH SPRING, OLD BROWN

Yamabushi of the Adirondacks,
stood beneath an icy waterfall
and washed his sheep, pulling burrs
and twigs from greasy fleece,
muttering a mutton mantra.

He led his flock through the hoof-rot pond,
awash in a sea of formaldehyde.
Each spring, Old Brown
moved his bed to the barn.

The newborn,
in their life-lust,
their brutal exuberance,
pulled the ewes inside out.

But Old Brown raised the dead,
with a fiery hand pushed back the uterus.
He carried limp lambs to the kitchen,
bathed them in the sink,
spoon-fed and swaddled them.

ETERNITY BEFORE, ETERNITY BEHIND

An eternity before, an eternity behind,
and we the little speck between,
little spark, dense dwarf star,
a nugget of light in a ring of fire.

I love you fierce, a marble heart.
I do not take you for granite.
I have crossed an ocean of time
to find you, to see you again
for the first time.

We the little speck
between the sheets,
nipple of light,
needle of light.
The hook is set,
hang me on your stringer.

LIKE CHARON CROSSING THE OHIO

After that first girl—I never did see her again—I never saw my passengers.
It would have to be the "black nights" of the moon when I would carry them,

and I would meet them out in the open or in a house without a single light.
The only way I knew who they were was to ask them, "What you say?"

And they would answer, "Menare." I don't know what that word meant—
it came from the Bible. I only know that was the password I used,

and all of them I took over told it to me before I took them.

VENUS OF THE ABATTOIR

The Great Sow is on the hoof.
She shoulders and snouts,
she is unstoppable.
We are nothing to her.

She is inedible, and she roots about,
chuff and snuff and chortle.
She pulls at the intestines like a thread.

This is meat science.
She is the size of a sofa,
too big to get up and eat.
She never sleeps, an eternally watchful monster.
What else is there to do but study the signs?
What else is there to do but assign meaning?

Venus of the Abattoir, who is like unto God?
We will hire a nobody to wipe your divine ass,
vestigial limbs shriveling beneath the weight of flesh.

Amelia Has Been Scalded to Death in an Accident Caused by Ruth

This is a bitter cup, indeed, but blessed be God:
a brighter day shall dawn; & let us not

sorrow as those that have no
hope. I humbly hope

this dreadful afflictive Providence
will lead us all more properly to appreciate

the amazing, unforeseen, untold,
consequences; that hang

upon the right or wrong doing of things seemingly of trifling account.

DEW FROM HEAVEN

—There were drops of blood on the corn like dew from heaven.

The corn is faceless, all ears and innuendo.
The rows are rigid, narrow, they forgive nothing,
green blinders, green chutes and blind alleys,
all ears, no mouths. Whisper and whatnot,
they give nothing away, kernels packed
with potentiality and primordial numbers,
a green suffocating sea, row's end an illusion.
All those ears and no mouths,
all those secrets and no lips to whisper.
They crucify scarecrows to their green gods.
As the dog backs away from the cornfield's edge
he growls, and in the corn, something growls back.

The Great Harvest

I felt for a number of years in earlier life:
a steady, strong, desire: to die: but since

I saw my prospect of becoming
a "reaper" in the great harvest

I have not only felt quite willing to live: but
have enjoyed life much & am now rather

anxious to live for a few years more.

HUNG BE THE HEAVENS

I

Hung be the Heavens in Scarlet!

I am Captain John Brown,
the defender of Osawatomie,
who swallows a Missourian whole,
and says grace after the meat,
the stone God threw
into the black pool of Slavery.

I am an iron angel black as a locomotive
and I have let go the wolf's ears.
I carry no scales and my heart is a broadsword,
my breath sours apples in the orchard.
I am Abaddon, Angel of the Bottomless Pit,
I lead you into temptation, deliver you from Evil.
I'll eat your bones for breakfast.

Mechanized Reaper, I am
Death on an industrial scale;
Death an assembly line, meat-packing plant,
sausage-grinder, a shining silo of fodder.
Death a cotton gin.
Let the dead bury the dead.

I am a Holy Roller, Allis-Chalmers,
the Great Stinging Sickle-Tail.
My vanity plate reads GDS HAMR.
There is blood on the corn, like dew from heaven.
There are naked orchards and broken wheatfields.
I need a body count to make my point.

II

All of my early days I could remember pictures.
On the leaves in the woods there were
hieroglyphs and numbers with the forms of men
in different attitudes, portrayed in blood.
I couldn't understand reading or writing,

27

I didn't read anything but the Bible and Camaro magazines.
But I could understand looking at a car or a motor,
or anything I could put my hands on.

I heard a loud noise in the heavens, a cosmic backfire.
And the Spirit appeared to me and said the Serpent was loosened,
and Christ had laid down the yoke He had borne for the sins of men,
and that I should take it on and fight against the Serpent,
for the time was fast approaching when
the first should be last and the last should be first.
I saw white spirits and black spirits engaged in battle,
and the sun was darkened, the thunder rolled in the heavens,
and blood flowed in streams, and I heard a voice saying,
'Such is your luck, such you are called to see, and let it
come rough or smooth, you must surely bear it.'
I saw my prospect of becoming a Reaper in the Great Harvest.

III

I am your Night Conductor, Shadow Man, Bridge Walker,
a Man of Constant Sorrow, of Wooden Horses and Riddles.
I am the Light at the Tunnel's End.
In Getty's town I sowed six million pounds of flesh,
my seed strewn across wheatfield and peach orchard.
Dead oxen breed bees, horses wasps, and beetles
rise out of asses. Human carcasses, when the marrow thickens,
produce serpents. Take them up.
There were seven thousand dead men.
There were three thousand dead horses.
Citizens soaked their handkerchiefs in penny-royal until Fall.

The Lincoln-Davis Cartage Company
promised "Metal Coffins Warranted Air-Tight,"
that could "be placed in the parlor without fear
of any odor escaping therefrom."
For one hundred dollars it would seem as though
the subject "had died on the day of arrival home."
Embalmers advertised their wares, preserved bodies
propped up like Burma Shave signs or sandwich boards,
unknown dead, souvenirs collected from the fields.
They died in every imaginable posture, common as Model T's.
One death is a tragedy; a million is a statistic.
Men were atomized by rotten-shot, maggots rioted
in sheer tonnage. Every fence and bush was black with flies,

every post and rail, not a crow or buzzard to be seen.

I am the flare that signals the train wreck,
a smudge pot flickering along the berm.
Hawk-eyed and hatchet-faced, I am
the weatherman you don't need,
the shepherd you shall not want.

LEVIATHAN

General Tubman opiates the babies,
carries a pistol in case anyone's will weakens.
Did ye know that the harpoon was invented
by an escaped slave, man with a heart of iron?
St. Elmo's Fire dances in the rigging,
dances like lighter fluid down the center of the road,
and the telephone's phantom jingle sounds like
sleigh bells in deep snow, the gray sea all around us.

Slavery is the American Leviathan, and we,
Jonahs all, rattle about inside its brass ribs.
Slavery is a lie white as a whale,
white as lice and cotton bolls,
white as a moccasin's mouth,
the South a bone church from stem to stern.

This is what ye have shipped for. To chase
that white whale on both sides of land, and over
all sides of the earth, till he spouts black blood
and rolls fin out. What say ye, will ye splice
hands on it now?

I dream its ghostly form in the watery twilight,
the underslung scissor of the jaw,
the house of the brow, rising.

LETTER FROM OLD BROWN REGARDING HARRIET TUBMAN

I am succeeding to all appearances
beyond my expectation. Hariet Tubman

hooked on his whole team at once.
He Hariet is the most of a man,

naturally; that I ever met with.

Just Like Saint Francis

Annie tried to tell the Captain she was ready to volunteer herself, but his attention seemed to be totally diverted by two tiny wrens that kept flying up to him and twittering in a kind of human anguish and anxiety. He told Annie the birds wanted something of him, were asking for help. He went off the porch to look for their nest and found a snake about to devour some fledglings. He killed the snake with a stick and came back smiling. The birds sat still and sang.

FIRE AND ICE

Every revolution requires deep pockets.
Old Brown was a money pit.

Soft as sow's teats, the Secret Six were men without fists.
They were pigeons who flew the coop.

Old Brown was an angel of light.

He was the lightning rod-maker, Doctor Boom
of the Burma Shave signs and battered broadsword.

He looked like a meat axe.

The boneless Brahmins stewed and spit like sparklers,
pledged Beecher's Bibles and bloodless emancipation.

Talk, talk, tick, tock, the metronomic patter
of their parlors and poster beds.

Old Brown was thunderstruck. He didn't
need a weatherman to know which way the wind blows.

He bombed The Thinker, blocked the engine house door.
At the red light he lit the fuse in the rental truck.

He held Oliver's hand as he died,
he let go the wolf's ears.

Letter Sent by Frederick Douglass

The Old Man is a wanton angel,
another white man with
a hat full of promises.
Another white man looking
for a second fiddle,
Tonto to his Lone Ranger.
The sort of man who
wants you to think
he knows something
you don't, his plans
bogus as a Feejee Mermaid.
Kimosabe, my black ass.
Does he think we are
five dusky phantoms
fresh formed out of air?
Like Belshazzar, he has seen
the handwriting on the wall
but, change blind, can't
read a word of it.
He should mind his own beeswax.
As Sophocles said,
"The swarm of the dead
hums and rises upward."
Who does he think I am?
I am no beekeeper shrouded in white.
I have stolen myself,
am both sign & signifier,
the snake who swallows
his own tail.

PANTS ON FIRE

I

I am no adventurer; you all know me; you are acquainted with my history, you know what I have done in Kansas. I do not expose my plans, nobody knows them but myself, except, perhaps one. I do not wish to be interrogated. If you wish to give me anything, I want you to give it freely. I have no other purpose but to serve the cause of liberty.

II

Every time I said "Kansas," I said "Slave" in my heart.

REGARDING POTTAWATOMIE

Old Brown only ever said four things:

I can only say about them that they had a perfect right to be hung.

I killed no man except in a fair fight.

I killed no innocent man.

God is my judge.

Nothing more. He was silent as a grave.

SLEEPER CELL, KENNEDY FARM HOUSE

*—Exert all your energy, for this is an opportunity that comes
once in a thousand years. All of you come back dead!*

The farm house is a thunder-besom,
a mutter at best, more sigh, or whisper.
Its lips are sutured. It's all need to know.
The neighbor lady leans on the front gate and squints
but the glass reflects nothing. The house
is a clenched jaw, teeth like broken windows.

Inside the boys rattle about, all bones and bread batter.
Their tongues are nailed to the gallows post.
Their thoughts are rented rooms.
Their feet are nailed to the floor.
Silence is tight as a belt, taut as a strop.
Annie calls them, "The Invisibles."
They believe they are going to make history.

They pick clean their combs,
coo like pigeons at vespers,
like monks in the rafters.
They assemble "Hoe Handles" and "Kitchen Tools,"
clutch axe handles and oaken pikes, antennae
that draw the darkening thunderheads,
thumbprint bruises of a terrible God.
And thunder shakes the panes like ghosts,
and thunder rumbles through the floor like caissons.

They shout with every spasm of lightning and thunder-boom,
dance through every splintering storm.
They squeal like pigs.
They are magicians' assistants, stiff as boards.
Old Brown passes his hand between their
severed torsos, nothingness up his sleeve,
his practiced patter a metallic clang.
Those boys didn't know the half of it.

ATOP HOG PEN GAP

> *—Paradise is beneath the shadow of the sword.*
> *Nothing is true and all is allowed.*

The Old Man fed us hashish and whiplash, bullshit and butter sauce,
and when he said, "Jump!" I said, "How high?"

We flew like cannonballs, dropped like amputations,
we fell through the trap door and were jerked to paradise.

That last step is a lulu.

Strap me up Boss, my thumb's on the detonator.
My hand is filled with punk and fat light.

BREAKING THE JAWS

He wanted to know if we were
willing to make common cause with him
in doing all in our power to
"break the jaws of the wicked
and pluck the spoil out of his teeth."
Would we apply the cattle prods.
Would we pry with pliers gold fillings from the molars.
Would we pile pyramids of eyeglasses, stack towers of suitcases.
Would we shave heads & stuff pillows, weave ropes of hair,
enough with which to hang ourselves.
Would we make mountains of skulls,
mountains of amputations.
Would we make mountains out of mole hills.
Would we make lampshades of skin,
grind bones to meal.
Would we cross T's, dye eyes.
Would we beat with brass knuckles & ballpeen hammers.
Would we throttle and hack.
Would there be broken glass.
Would there be cattle cars.
Would there be racks of scalps.
Would we tip helicopters over the gray Atlantic,
pack rental trucks with explosives.
Would we build a Bone Church.
Would we drop the canister down the chute.
Would we count each nose, each foreskin and necklace of ears.
Would we weigh each pound of flesh.
Would we neatly and solemnly log
each & every entry in God's Red Totenbuch.
Would we take plenty of pictures.

MAPS OF NEVERLAND

I

It's those siren songs that bring it to mind.
The one swimming beneath the other, passing like
a fish, palimpsest, like maps of Neverland.
The Battle Hymn, loosed and trampling, marches on,
while John Brown, one trick pony,
molders underground, jelly on the riverbottom,
dead fish throbbing in God's hillock,
soil from which the grapes of wrath were grown.

There are zigzag lines on Neverland,
like your temperature on a card, like sutures,
whip lash, or the seams of crazy quilts.
These are probably roads on the island.
Every crossroad is called Blackhead Signpost.

It would be an easy map if that were all. But there are also
flaming monks, unmarked graves, fairies who slip change beneath the pillow,
submarines crushed like eggshells beneath tons of darkness,
the burst head of a president, and water snakes that wriggle like Moses' staff.
When the Thresher implodes and there's no one there to listen,
does it make a sound?

There are pallbearers and purple funeral flags
that flutter stiffly from fenders, mushroom clouds
and shadows annealed to sidewalks; chin music, stepping
in the bucket, burlap bags of drowned kittens.
There are iron lungs, black ice, and fairy loops.
There are pyramids of limbs, fields that wriggle in the twilight,
and blasted trees stripped of leaves. There are the fun house
livingrooms of funeral homes, the dead like davenports.
There's black face and high yellow, and money in Master's pocket.
There are construction paper maps of the states.
There's shop class and fistfights in the Armory parking lot.

There's leg braces' wingnuts and built-up shoes,
duck and cover, hammer and sickle, fateful lightning.
There are broken zippers and galoshes buckles,
the climbing rope that hangs like a noose.
There is a snowplane hurtling down stubbled cornfields,
a dog that circles above us, a man eaten by hogs,
a rowboat firing a cannon over the drowned
to draw them to the river's surface.
And either these are part of the island,
or they are another map showing through,
and it is all rather confusing, especially as nothing will stand still.
Sometimes there are mountains like God's bower.
Sometimes there are rivers choked with stairwells of ice.

II

Nothing is what it seems. That mountain there—
maybe it wasn't there yesterday and won't be
there tomorrow. You get to the point where
you're not even sure it is a mountain.

III

When you play at it by day with chairs and tablecloth,
Neverland is not the least alarming, but in the two minutes
before sleep it becomes very nearly real.

The Neverland had always begun to look a little dark
and threatening by bedtime. Then unexplored patches
arose in it and spread; black shadows moved about in them.
You lost the certainty that you would win.

Lost Boys

The Old Man would come down laughing
over something fearfully funny
he had been saying to a star,
but he had already forgotten what it was,
or he would come up with mermaid scales
still sticking to him, and yet not be able
to say for certain what had been happening.

His courage was almost appalling.

The boys on the island varied, of course, in numbers,
as they got killed and so on; and when
they grew up, which is against the rules,
the Old Man thinned them out.

It was only in the Old Man's absence
that they could speak of mothers.
They wore the skins of bears slain by themselves,
in which they were so round and furry
that when they fell they rolled.
They therefore became very sure-footed.

Unless your tree fitted you it was
difficult to go up and down,
and no two of the boys were quite the same size.
But you simply must fit,
and the Old Man measured you for your tree
as carefully as for a suit of clothes;
the only difference being that the clothes are made to fit you,
while you have to be made to fit the tree.
Only Douglass refused to fit. And Harriet refused to fit.

Usually it was done quite easily,
as by wearing too many garments or too few;
but if you were bumpy in awkward places
or the only available tree was an odd shape,
the Old Man did some things to you,
and after that you fit.

Once you fit, great care
must be taken to go on fitting.
After a few day's practice
they could go up and down the trunks
as gaily as buckets in a well.

But Harriet was no Tinker Bell bewitched by Pan.
She didn't need a Weatherman to know which way the wind blows.
The Old Man had seen many tragedies,
but he had forgotten them all.
He gnashed his pretty teeth with joy.

He stopped circling, stayed in one place.
Everything should have come around.

OLD BROWN PILOTS AN OHKA

I skim the Shenandoah like a dragonfly.

God's mouth is a cockpit
fragrant with cherry blossoms.

The Ohka is algebraic
at four hundred miles per hour,
nose smooth as the cosmic egg.
There are captive after-images;
fingerprints' galaxies just beneath
the surface, like in a new car showroom.

Do the math. It's all I can manage
to hold on. Time collapses, ideogrammatic.
I have eaten sea bream, dried abalone,
chestnuts and seaweed.
I am sign and signifier.
Disgrace does not trouble me.
My errors were decreed
before the world was made.

I am a Thunder God, an Earthshaker,
I skim the blue water like a dragonfly.
The gun deck will run with blood,
knee-caps, scalps, tongues and arms.
Obligation is heavy as a mountain,
death lighter than a feather.

Each November I shall descend to shadowy
Appalachia, the sky a faceless scrim,
to one of twelve musty god-houses.
Crows will leap, leaving kanji in the snow.
All my houses are empty, all is done,
and I can nap for a million years.

The Moon Was Just Right

Kagi thought "the moon was just right" because slaves were more discontented after the crops had been harvested than at any other season. And a slave man had hung himself a few days ago when his wife was sold away.

A "right moon" and a hanging black man.

These were good signs.

I declare that War is now being waged.

Listen. There is no choice left but to defend life by all and every means possible against the genocidal machine.

Do not be deceived. It is a classic strategem of genocide to camouflage their wars as law and order police actions.

Remember the Sioux and the Jews and black slaves and the marijuana progroms and pious TWA indignation over hijackings.

Listen Americans. Your government is an instrument of total lethal evil.

Remember the buffalo and the Iroquois!

Remember Kennedy, King, Malcolm, Lenny.

Listen. There is no compromise with a machine. You cannot talk peace and love to a humanoid robot whose every Federal bureaucratic impulse is soulless, heartless, lifeless, loveless.

In this life struggle we use the ancient holy strategies of organic life.

Resist lovingly in the loyalty of underground sisterhoods and brotherhoods.

Resist passively, break lock step. Drop out.

Resist actively, sabotage, jam the Gin. Hijack trains. Trash every lethal machine in the land.

Resist publicly, announce life. Denounce death.

Resist privately, guerilla invisibility.

Resist beautifully, create organic art, music.

Resist biologically, be healthy. Erotic. Conspire with the seed. Breed.

Resist spiritually, praise God. Love life. Blow the mechanical mind with Holy Acid. Dose them. Dose them.

Resist physically, robot agents who threaten life must be disarmed, disabled, disconnected by force. Arm yourself and shoot to live. Life is never violent. To shoot a genocidal robot policeman in the defense of life is a sacred act.

II

HUNTING

In the hunt, as in Calvinism,
it is over before it even begins.
The only question is how it will occur.
The young raiders are Djinn,
fifty caliber angels stripped to the bone.
They embrace the firefight's liberating clarity
—keep your powder dry, your rifle clean—
politics and philosophy dead as doornails.
Theirs is a landscape gone red.
They are out of the bottle, blooded hunters
daubed with the sticky first kill,
Owen hacking with a broadsword,
Sadie Mae Glutz with a fork in her hand,
each of them with consciences clean as Saint Michael's.
Those boys are walls of testosterone
who've thrust a finger in the socket.
Quakers with carbines, faces flush with combat,
they sport angelic elegance,
it enfolds them, a holy flak jacket.
They've recognized the obvious beauty
of the kill, its simplicity, and so
they flame like gods or hot rods, their hair on fire.
They shriek, auto-da-fe, dance and hop
and stand on one leg like Kali, peel the face
off Sambo, and unshackle the Mau Mau beneath.
They would count foreskins if the Old Man asked it.
This is what they've been made for
since before they were born.
They have never been so alive.

TELEGRAM FROM HARPERS FERRY

NEGRO INSURRECTION AT HARPER'S FERRY, VIRGINIA—
SEIZURE OF THE UNITED STATES ARSENAL BY THE INSUR-
RECTIONISTS—EXTENSIVE NEGRO CONSPIRACY IN VIRGIN-
IA AND MARYLAND—BRIDGE TO HARPER'S FERRY FROM
MARYLAND FORTIFIED AND DEFENDED BY CANNON—
TRAINS FIRED INTO AND STOPPED—TELEGRAPH WIRES
CUT—CONTRIBUTIONS LEVIED ON CITIZENS—SEVEN HUN-
DRED AND FIFTY BLACK AND WHITE ABOLITIONISTS HOLD
ARSENAL AND GUN WORKS—EVERY LIGHT IN TOWN IS EX-
TINGUISHED AND THE HOTELS ARE CLOSED—ALL ROADS
LEADING THERE ARE BARRICADED AND GUARDED—WAG-
ONLOADS OF MUSKETS BEING SENT TO THE MOUNTAINS
IN MARYLAND—ADDING NEW FLAMES TO THE FIRES OF
EXCITEMENT THE NAME OF THE LEADER IS OSAWATOMIE
BROWN—BROWN EXPECTS REINFORCEMENTS OF FIFTEEN
HUNDRED MEN BY TOMORROW MORNING—THE BAGGAGE
MASTER OF THE MAIL TRAIN COMING IN FROM THE WEST
WAS TAKEN PRISONER AND CARRIED INTO THE ARMORY
WHERE HE FOUND SIX HUNDRED NEGROES AND TWO OR
THREE HUNDRED WHITE MEN IN ARMS—ALMOST ALL THE
LEADING CITIZENS OF HARPER'S FERRY ARE HELD AS HOS-
TAGES—

Monument to Heyward Shepard

"On the night of October 16, 1858
Heyward Shepard, an industrious
and respected colored freeman,
was mortally wounded by John
Brown's raiders in pursuance
of his duties as an employee of
the Baltimore and Ohio Railroad
Company. He became the first
victim of this attempted
insurrection.

This boulder is erected by
The United Daughters of the
Confederacy and the Sons of
Confederate Veterans as a
memorial to Heyward Shepard,
exemplifying the character and
faithfulness of thousands of
Negroes who, under many
temptations throughout
subsequent years of war, so
conducted themselves that
no stain was left upon a record
which is the peculiar heritage
of the American people, and an
everlasting tribute to the best
in both races."

EDWIN & BARCLAY COPPOC

—I felt special, excited, chosen.

I

The Coppoc brothers were fatherless boys whose gentleness
and decency were the pride of their widowed mother's heart.
They were reared on a farm southwest of Salem, Ohio,
near the present TV relay tower. When a letter from Chambersburg
summoned the "miners," like turn-spit dogs curtailed the boys
told their Mother they were headed back to flat Ohio,
The Western Reserve, Satan's Seat, black heart of abolition.
They might as well have said they were headed to Oz in a tornado.

Ohio? I believe you are going with Old Brown.
When you get halters round your necks, will you think of me?

Mother, when Uncle Charley fixes his eye on you
and says you have to come, you have to come.

Just ask Watson, Squeaky, or Sadie Mae Glutz.
Charley has a broadsword in his dune buggy,
counts the foreskins of his enemies.

Uncle Charley rhymes, he chimes,
You won't get caught if you don't have a thought.
He says, *No sense makes sense.*
He says, *You can't kill kill.*
And we believe him.

II

Edwin Coppoc was manacled to Old Brown,
common thief, simple sinner to the Old Man's
Christ, his apotheosis. Nothing more than
a lapsed Quaker who shot Mayor Beckham
as he peered around the water tank,
then huffed and puffed,
That's one little piggy down!

Unlike the Old Man, he did not
make of the gallows a cross.

When Edwin shot Mayor Beckham,
the Quaker's buck & ball freed Beckham's slaves,
whose will provided for manumission
upon his death. At that moment
it began to rain.

lll

At 4:00 Coppock shot and killed Mayor Fontaine Beckham.
Edwin Coppoc fired twice at the Mayor.
It was the second bullet killed him. A magic bullet.
Beckham had been distressed by the fatal shooting during the night
of his baggage assistant, Shepard, whose wife and three children
Beckham had recently purchased intending one day to set them free.

The death of Mayor Beckham in plain view
drove the crowd into a frenzy, which resulted
in the murder of Will Thompson, dragged from the Gault Hotel.
Shot with pistols, his body was shoved between the ties
of the B&O bridge and dropped like a crash dummy
into the gray river.

Coppock drew a bead on Colonel Lee but a hostage,
Jesse W. Graham (who relates this story),
begged him not to shoot.
Edwin could have put a slug through History's heart,
torn flesh and the fabric of time and space,
though we'd never have known it, it being
just an obscure officer who bled out
in the armory yard.

Another hostage, named Ball, said the man who shot Beckham
was killed when the marines stormed the building.
My, how they lightninged and thundered.

Barclay was at large.

IV

Because Edwin was hanged,
he came home on the government's dime,
to the cemetery called "Hope,"
and a grave layered in dirt & straw.

Edwin told a reporter that he had not wanted
to come to Harper's Ferry and
had no idea it would result in treason.
He'd never handled a gun.

I am thankful that no one fell by my hands, he said.

The trial was whisked away in a morning.
It was not extensively reported:

"Edwin Coppock, one of John Brown's men, hanged at Harpers Ferry,
December 16, 1859. The body of this martyr to the anti-slavery cause
was sent to the home of his relatives living near New Garden—
though now it's called Winona—and on December 18
it was buried in the Friends' burying ground of that small village,
in the presence of as many as two thousand witnesses."

For two weeks the grave was guarded
against Copperheads and Resurrection Men,
then re-interred, at Hope, in an unusually deep grave.
They say six thousand people
filed past that plain, black walnut coffin.

Only Edwin's not actually buried under his sandstone shaft
but some rods to the southwest of the monument,
some say across the road. They say the body's
encased in 40 tons of sandstone.

DOMINION

The Old Man paces the engine room like David in the wilderness.
He mimics the raccoon's chitter, the coyote's yodel.
He mimics crows with voices like pump handles.
His face is wrinkled as a bloodhound's,
every molecule trembles.
His mind is lifted upon the updraft,
circles like the red-tailed hawk,
threads a maze of currents and eddies.
He coddles the fallen sparrow,
fingers mud-dauber's panpipes.
He causes the red-winged blackbirds to rise
and fall, their shoulders on fire.
He is a mockingbird. He clamps
onto an idea like a snapping turtle.
The walking stick clings to him,
the mantis prays to him.
His thoughts are like geese
pulling winter in behind them.
He whistles the groundhog from his burrow,
draws the star-nosed mole to the surface.
He alone knows the earthworm's sex.
His mind is a pasture blinking with fireflies.
His heart is like a rabbit,
like a fox trotting along the turnpike.
When cicadas sing their saw-song
he is busy as a wasp.
There is a terrible gathering in his head,
clouds of starlings. His skull
is raw and red as a vulture's.

WHEN THE BEES DIDN'T HIVE

When the bees didn't hive, Old Brown was pole-axed.
It hit him like a ton of bricks, like a Mack truck.

Only nobody took down the license plate.

Suddenly there were no bees in his bonnet.
His mind was a deer caught in the headlights.
His mind was an empty magician's box.
His mind was a hollow hive
still as a station wagon on its roof,
still and square on the centerline.

There was no there there.
There were no bees in his bonnet.

Stolen bees will die,
and swarms fortell misfortune.

Old Brown was rigid, change blind and brittle as iron.
Mene, Mene, Tekel, Upharsin.
Stiff as a magician's assistant,
he couldn't read the handwriting on the wall.
Mene, Mene, Tekel, Upharsin.
There it was. And wasn't.
Written by the disembodied
fingers of a man's hand.

There were no bees. No bonnet.

PIETA AND POST-MORTEM

I

The engine room was the size of a two-car garage.
Packed with hostages, it smelled of burnt powder and flop-sweat.
Every single window was destroyed, and the bullet holes
made trails, like a celestial star map.

His boy gut-shot, Old Brown sputtered and fumed,
paced in the darkness, thumping like Ahab,
whispering to himself and crying out,
Men, are you awake?

Watson lay limp as Christ on the engine room floor,
gun smoke thick as incense. The Old Man stood over him.
Die, if you must, grumbled Old Brown, hatchet-faced mother.
He was a raw nerve.

II

He asked to be dispatched, or killed, or put out of his misery,
or something of that kind, I think, and Brown remarked to him,
No my son, have patience; I think you will get well; if you die,
you die in a glorious cause, fighting for liberty, or freedom, or
something like that.

III

Medical students snatched Watson's body,
crammed it into a barrel and carted it
to Winchester Medical College where
he was field-dressed like a rabbit,
and the skin varnished, after which
a dispute arose whether he should be
stuffed by a taxidermist or cut up
into game pouches and coin purses.

Instead, he became a Visible Man,
with nerves like blue highways,
and vessels like rivers of blood.
Four of his fingers and all the toes
were cut off by relic seekers,

as though he were a saint
or their favorite celebrity.

IV
An eyewitness, one of the captive men, said:

With one son dead by his side,
and another shot through,
he felt the pulse of his dying son
with one hand, and held his rifle
with the other, and commanded his men
with the utmost composure, encouraging them
to be firm, and to sell their lives
as dear as they could.

Thoreau cited this, and so it must be true.

DANGERFIELD NEWBY'S EARS

—I'm your worst nightmare, a nigger with a gun.

Dangerfield Newby's ears
were bat wings on the barn floor,
bowling trophy in the closet,
black butterflies in a mason jar.
They fluttered against the glass walls
like moths who batter porch door screens.
They groaned like ebony oboes.
They were cornucopias of horror,
or little wings of prophecy,
whittled shavings of mahogany,
black sea shells in a jar,
licorice twists, tobacco plugs,
educational souvenirs from Ol' Virginny.
They were fodder for poker night follies.
They were black as church bells in the belfry,
sharp as obsidian, sinister as Malcom's X,
black flames guttering in the
alluvial darkness of the closet.
They were tubes of quivering black light,
bits of tire, dried plums,
gravy-train crayfish, black curd,
black crescents congealed as Turkish coffee,
were caramel chewy and smelled like tar.

The King of Terrors himself could not exceed those hogs

in zealous attention to the
defunct Newby.

They tugged away at him with might and main,

and this writer saw one   run its snout into his wound

and drag out a stringy substance   of some kind,

which he is not anatomist enough   to call by its right name.

It appeared to be very long or elastic,

one end being in the hog's mouth

and the other in the man's body.

AGAPE

For Oliver Brown and Dangerfield Newby

—Sacrificial love is not based on a feeling,
but a determined act of the will.

The militia who killed them,
men dead in trespasses and sin,
rolled them into a common grave.

There was nothing common about it.

Someone arranged their arms in embrace,
tucked them in like sweethearts,
like delicate birds.

But these were ironclad angels.
This was love to the point of death.

The mob meant to mock them, of course.
Might as well have jammed crowns
of thorns upon their heads.

The mob can only mock,
monkey see, monkey do,
their collective brain shrunk
small as a boiled peanut.

Hold on tight, we tell our children
as the bar drops and the rollercoaster begins.

Oliver is a shaft of light on a dark field,
Dangerfield a lighthouse in troubled waters.

They are radiant spears of light,
phosphorescent pikes that glow like St. Elmo's fire,
like the green aura of a shallow grave.

They turn and burn to the bone,
buried on the bank of the Shenandoah.

Old Brown in the Cyclops' Cave

Old Brown's raid was a poke in the eye with a sharp stick.
The Cyclops groped blindly for insight. He cast stones.
Old Brown lay on the jailhouse floor, skeleton key,
his beard caked with blood. The Cyclops roared,
Mr. Brown, who sent you here?
The Old Man bared his teeth, face gunpowder black.
He looked like a man cut away from the stake.
No man sent me here. It was my own prompting
and that of my Maker, or of the devil, whichever
you wish to ascribe it to. I acknowledge
no master in human form.

Old Brown took his men into death's cave mouth.
Maddened by abolition's sirens,
he wrecked his crew at every turn.
His men were eaten alive in the streets.
Pigs rooted in their bowels for explanations and secrets.
His men floated in the shallows, shot to pieces,
were skinned and varnished. There were
no fat sheep to cling to, no one cast a blind eye.
It was easier to get in than to get out.

Jeremiah Anderson: Bayoneted by a Marine against the rear wall of the engine-house. You could have spun him like a pinwheel. Died immediately. Winchester Medical College staff took his body away for anatomical study.

Watson Brown: Showered with bullets while carrying a white flag of truce. He crawled back to the engine-house, shot in the bowels. Pulled inside by his brother, Oliver, he vomited blood. Died the next day. Winchester Medical College staff took his body for a museum specimen.

Oliver Brown: Shot in the chest at the engine-house doorway kneeling to fire. Choking and crying, the brothers died at their father's feet, side by side on the floor.

John Henry Kagi: Killed while trying to lead his men in an escape across the Shenandoah River. Died in the water.

Lewis Leary: Retreating across the Shenandoah River he received a mortal gunshot wound to the back. Copeland dragged him out to a rock in midstream. Leary lingered until the next day, then died in a cooper's shop in Harpers Ferry after begging reporters to write a farewell message to his wife and infant son.

Jim: Clubbed and drowned in the river.

William Leeman: Ran across the armory yard and leaped over a gate. Was seen scrambling through a culvert beneath the yard and came under heavy fire as he emerged at the riverbank. Started to wade the Potomac River to the Maryland side, was spotted and followed out to a rock in the river. "*Don't shoot! I surrender!*" Leeman cried. Armory worker George Schoppert leveled his pistol and smiled. He shot Leeman in the head at point-blank range. He blew away Leeman's face. The body lay on the rock for hours, used for target practice. Bullet-ridden, it eventually slid into the water and floated off.

Dangerfield Newby: Shot through the neck with a six-inch spike. Townspeople poked sticks into the wound. Newby's ears and genitals were cut off as souvenirs. Townspeople abused his body for hours, then left him in the street for wandering hogs to rip apart and eat.

Stewart Taylor: Shot in the forehead in the engine-house doorway. Died instantly.

Dauphin Thompson: Bayoneted by a Marine as he crawled, skulking, under a fire engine. Died a few hours later.

William Thompson: Captured under a white flag. When Coppock killed the mayor, George Chambers and Henry Hunter burst into the Wager House and stormed upstairs to seize Thompson. The mob dragged him outside, kicking and screaming, to the B&O Bridge, where they shot him with revolvers and he slipped into the Potomac. As he clung to a bridge support, townspeople spotted him and shot him to death. The mob continued to shoot at his body all afternoon. He could be seen, face up on the river bottom, for a day or two after.

John Cook: Captured by slave hunters near Mont Alto, PA. Returned to Harpers Ferry, tried, convicted, and hanged.

John Copeland: Attempted to escape across the Shenandoah. Was stranded on a rock in the middle of the river. A local man, James H. Holt, waded towards Copeland, pointed his rifle at him, and pulled the trigger. At the same time, Copeland tried to shoot back. Both rifles were wet and did not fire. Both pulled pistols, and again, they did not fire. Holt made it to the rock, the shivering Copeland surrendered, and Holt led him ashore. He was tried, convicted, and hanged. The judge said he'd have let him go, if he could. Dug up less than an hour after burial for dissection by students from Winchester Medical College.

Edwin Coppoc: Captured by Marines in the engine-house. Tried, convicted, and hanged.

Shields Green: Captured by Marines in the engine-house. Tried, convicted, and hanged. Buried in a mass grave on the banks of the Shenandoah. Dug up less than an hour later for dissection by students from Winchester Medical College.

Albert Hazlett: Slipped into the crowd and escaped in a boat across the Potomac. Captured near Carlisle, PA, and extradited to Virginia. Tried, convicted, and hanged.

Aaron Stevens: Shot four times while carrying a flag of truce. Recovered from his wounds, was tried, convicted, and hanged.

Ben: Arrested and jailed without charge, where he was said to have died of fright.

MEDIA AND MAD VISIONS

The Old Man had laid hands
upon Sumner's blood-stiff waistcoat.
Its electricity passed through him like copperheads,
and he prophesized like a Delphic outlet:
The angels of God are walking up and down the streets,
marking the deeds of men.
From behind the jailhouse door, he spoke through vines of extension cords
spliced and duct-taped to the floor. Cats played with the sutures
and dogs chewed at his words.

The girls circled on the sidewalks of Charleston,
shaved their heads like monks or turkey vultures,
carved swastikas with steak knives to mark the site
of their elusive third eye, skinny white kids from the heartland,
homicidal in the name of Helter Skelter.
Every time the Old Man took a drink from in his monkish cell,
water dropped in the tumbler centered in their sacred hoop,
their wobbly gyroscope, its orbit in decay.

The Old Man sacrificed his sons like a Canaanite.
They died all about him, buckshot and bayoneted,
pinioned to the wall like porkers.
A great gray magnet, he drew iron filings:
the blade of Frederick the Great,
Israel Green's bent dress sword,
a machete sheathed in a dune buggy.

He glared like steel from the cover of Time.
Bullets, he said, *should be free as words.*
Network vans clustered like blowflies. There were packs
of newshounds and flashbulb paparazzi.
Their wordstreams ricocheted off satellites
in the stupefying silence.

I have, may it please the court, a few words to say.

In the first place, I deny everything but what I have all along admitted: of a design on my part to free the slaves. I intended certainly to have made a clean thing of that matter, as I did last winter, when I went into Missouri and there took slaves without the snapping of a gun on either side, moving through the country, and finally leaving them in Canada. I designed to have done the same thing on a larger scale. That was all I intended. I never did intend murder, or treason, or the destruction of property, or to excite or incite slaves to rebellion, or to make insurrection.

I have another objection, and that it is unjust that I should suffer such a penalty. Had I interfered in the manner which I admit, and which I admit has been fairly proved—for I admire the truthfulness and candor of the greater portion of the witnesses who have testified in this case—had I so interfered in behalf of the rich, the powerful, the intelligent, the so-called great, or in behalf of any of their friends, whether father, mother, brother, sister, wife, or children, or any of that class, and suffered and sacrificed what I have in this interference, it would have been all right. Every man in this Court would have deemed it an act worthy of reward rather than punishment.

This Court acknowledges, too, as I suppose, the validity of the law of God. I see a book kissed, which I suppose to be the Bible, or at least the New Testament, which teaches me that all things whatsoever I would that men should do to me, I should do even so to them. It teaches me, further, to remember them that are in bonds as bound with them. I endeavored to act up to that instruction. I am yet too young to understand that God is any respecter of persons. I believe that to have interfered as I have done, as I have always freely admitted I have done, in behalf of His despised poor, I did no wrong, but right. Now if it is deemed necessary that I should forfeit my life for the furtherance of the ends of justice, and mingle my blood further with the blood of millions in this slave country whose rights are disregarded by wicked, cruel, and unjust enactments, I say, let it be done.

LETTER FROM MAHALA DOYLE OF POTTAWATOMIE, KANSAS

I do feel gratified, to hear that you were stopped in your fiendish career at Harper's Ferry, with the loss of your two sons, you can now appreciate my distress in Kansas, when you entered my house at midnight and arrested my Husband and two boys, and took them out of the yard and in cold blood shot them dead in my hearing, you cant say you done it to free slaves, we had none and never expected to own one, but has only made me a poor disconsolate widow with helpless children. O how it pained my heart to hear the dying groans of my Husband & children.

SECRET SIX

Every revolution requires deep pockets,
financiers sketchy as a Feejee Mermaid.
Old Brown called them men without fists,
but he took their money:

Theodore Parker: One of the nation's best-known preachers.
The Billy Graham of his day. Fled to Canada.

Gerritt Smith: Former Congressman and millionaire. Father had been
John Jacob Astor's partner. Had a mental collapse upon hearing of John
Brown's capture. Five days after the execution, he was committed to the
New York State Asylum for the Insane in Utica.

Samuel Gridley Howe: Boston philanthropist known for his work with
the deaf, blind, and mentally impaired. Known philanderer. Wife is Julia
Ward Howe, who wrote "The Battle Hymn of the Republic" to the tune
of "John Brown's Body." Fought in Greek revolution and with the Polish
rebels. Fled to Canada.

Franklin Benjamin Sanborn: Almost every dollar raised for the Old Man
passed through Sanborn's hands. More than $100,000. When a US
Marshal with a murder warrant was looking for Old Brown in Cleveland,
Sanborn took the Old Man to the home of a Boston judge, Thomas B.
Russell, for concealment. After the raid, Sanborn spent two nights
burning letters and manuscripts, then fled to Canada.

Thomas Wentworth Higginson: Stood his ground, remained in the
country, refused to destroy his letters, and defied anyone to arrest him.
Led a colored regiment. Became Emily Dickinson's literary executor.

George Luther Stearns: Suffered chronic bronchitis, wore a long beard
to protect his chest. Commissioned a white marble bust of Old Brown
while he awaited execution. Long a fixture in the Stearns' mansion, it was
compared by many to Michelangelo's "Moses." James Redpath said that it
might well be Moses, but it sure as hell wasn't Old Brown. Fled to Canada.

Brown kept letters revealing their complicity in a carpetbag at the Kennedy
house base camp. There were bushels of them.

FUNERAL OF EDWIN COPPOCK

The friends of Edwin Coppock and of the great principles of freedom for which HE sacrificed his life, and to advance which he suffered martyrdom, being desireous of showing proper respect to his memory have obtained his remains from his relatives, and have made arrangements to inter the body in the cemetery in

SALEM, FRIDAY, DECEMBER 30, 1859.

To meet at the TOWN HALL at 1 o'clock P.M. All friends of JUSTICE, LIBERTY and HUMANITY are invited to attend and participate in these solemn rites.

The historic value of the rude box in which it had come had been recognized by Dr. J.C. Whinnery, and he had preserved it in the attic of the building in which his offices were located. This fact was known to the writer of these lines and with the assistance of three others (young men) it was brought down and an effigy of General Lee was place in it. It had not been forgotten that it was General Lee who commanded the marines who broke into the Fort at Harper's Ferry, who prevented the escape of Edwin Coppock and were thus immediately responsible for his death. With this upon their shoulders they came out upon the street and in an incredibly short time they were marching at the head of a procession numbering more than a thousand people, all shouting the refrain of that great war hymn:

John Brown's body lies a moldering in his grave,
His soul goes marching on.

On Friday, the 30th of December, the remains of Edwin Coppock were exhumed at New Garden, brought to Salem, and placed in the town hall where they lay in state for an hour or two, and where they were viewed by about six thousand people. In the afternoon the remains were conveyed to their last resting place, followed by a long procession of citizens and strangers, colored and white, on foot and in vehicles. In a few days we shall publish a biographical sketch of Edwin Coppock including his imprisonment, his attempted escape, his execution, and the removal of his remains first to New Garden and then to Salem.

On Friday night, the 30th of December, and the next morning, the temperature fell about thirty degrees in fifteen hours. Saturday morning the thermometer indicated six degrees below zero.

On Saturday, December 31, 1859, a number of the dignified and usually sedate citizens of Salem drove about town in a large sleigh, making calls on their female friends who, with darkened parlors and refreshments, were waiting to receive them.

LETTER FROM MRS. RUSSELL

I

Brown said little about the raid, suggesting only that something had gone very wrong—that something had been done that he had expressly forbidden—and adding a few sharp words about "the famous Mr. Frederick Douglass," who, he said, had ruined a great opportunity. Of his sons who had died—he merely said that they had not been gently killed.

II

He could form beautiful dreams of things, as they should occur, and forthwith go into action on the basis of those dreams, making no sufficient allowance for some things occurring as they should not. John Brown's dreams were not always practical. But we loved and trusted John Brown.

THEM WOMEN LOVED OLD BROWN

—If you don't win in the bedroom, son, you're not going
to win on the battlefield.

Them women loved Old Brown, that Billy-Goat,
that great white whale, yellow Ticonderoga number two.
He was stiff as a spindle. His staff wriggled like a serpent.

***

Old Brown presented 16 year-old Mary with a written offer of marriage.
Mary put the note under her pillow and slept on it a night before opening.
After reading it, she rushed off to a spring to fetch water. Brown followed.
By the time they returned he had the answer he wanted.
He Moses, she a burning bush.

***

On the lam from Federal Marshals, he hid in Judge Russell's mansion in
Boston. At night before retiring he checked the loads in his revolvers,
once commenting, *Here are eighteen lives,* and, *I should hate to spoil these*
carpets, but you know I cannot be taken alive. Such melodrama. Such theatre.
Mrs. Russell called him a funnyman, a regular knee-slapper,
a real hoot, like on Big Chuck & Hoolihan,
his stories laced with black humor
bitter as strychnine or embalming fluid.

***

Females are susceptible of being carried away entirely by the kindness
of an intrepid and magnanimous soldier, even when his brave name
was but a terror the previous day.

***

One woman wrote to The Old Man in multi-colored ink,
letters gone a riotous runic, a rainbow code, excruciating,
needles to the eyes, all sign and no signification:
violet traffic signal, blue stop sign.

***

Those runaways from the Spahn Ranch
slipped the noose around America's neck.
Pulled the wool over her eyes.
Pulled the pillowcase over her head.

***

The celebrated writer and nonresistant abolitionist whom he had never met,
asked Governor Wise for permission to visit Brown in order
to *dress his wounds,* and *speak soothingly to him.*
She petted and fawned. She wanted to thrust her finger
through the holes in his palms.

***

One beauty, a Bond Girl no doubt, perhaps Pussy Galore, was urged to
charm her way into OB's cell where, while kissing the Old Man, she would
slip into his mouth a paper outlining plans for his rescue.

***

Mary cut from his letters sentences praising her or expressing regard,
put them away among her keepsakes, tucked them like peas beneath her
mattress, left his letters windowed with gaps through which you could
see her heart.

St. Albans

I was there. The funeral took place at one o'clock. The coffin was placed on a table brought outside and put beside the door. When the lid was taken off, the Old Man's face appeared faintly flushed, almost radiant. He glowed like Christ. His stare followed us about the room. The last words spoken over his casket were, *I have fought the good fight. I have finished my course. I have kept the faith.*

YOU CAN'T MAKE THIS STUFF UP

Asked, *What's all this fuss about, anyhow?*
the first thing a raider said to anyone was,
Oh, it's a Darkey affair. I am one and here's another.

The first man the raiders killed was Heyward Shepard,
B & O baggage handler shot in the back.
Heyward Shepard was a black man.

The Daughters of the Confederacy erected a monument
to Heyward Shepard.

The commanding officer of the Marines was Colonel Robert
Edward Lee, not yet the demi-god "Marse Robert,"
or post-war college president.

The junior officer who delivered the ultimatum for surrender into
Old Brown's hands was J.E.B. Stuart, sans plume, yellow kerchief,
and Puss & Boots boots.

Lt. Green bent his dress sword when he tried to skewer the Old Man.
He was one tough bird.

Cook wanted to give George Washington's stolen sword to
Frederick Douglass.

Two marines were killed. Lt. Green couldn't remember their names.

Osborne Anderson, only surviving raider from inside the armory,
said at least thirty militia men were killed.

Gut-shot, Watson Brown crawled to the engine-house doors.
Joseph Brua, one of the hostages walked out, lifted him up,
and carried him to the Wager House. Then he returned to the
engine-house and resumed his place with the hostages.

The commanding officer who supervised the Old Man's hanging
was Thomas Jackson, a professor of artillery at VMI,
before he became a stone wall, was estranged from his arm.

In the ranks of the 1st Virginia, in a borrowed uniform, stood
J.W. Booth, not yet the first presidential assassin; having not yet
yelled, *Sic semper tyrannis!* from the Ford Theatre stage.

In a uniform borrowed from the VMI cadets stood Edwin Ruffin,
who would fire the first shot on Fort Sumter.

The hangman's name was U.B. Dangling.

When his surrender was announced, an effigy of Lee was paraded
around Salem in the wagon that carried Coppock's coffin.

Julia Ward Howe, who wrote "Battle Hymn of the Republic" to the
tune of "John Brown's Body," was wife of Samuel Gridley Howe, one of
the Secret Six. The song began as a joke, "Say Hummers Will You Meet
Us?," first sung to entertain fire-eaters in South Carolina.

The Old Man had to stand on the gallows for around ten minutes.
His courage was almost appalling.

He fell about two feet. He wore red slippers.

He gave Green and Copeland 25 cents each.

Edwin Coppoc claimed that during two days in November, more than
800 people visited the jail.

Governor Wise claimed that he received 3,600 letters threatening rescue
during the sixty days Old Brown was in jail.

John Brown, Jr. left the service in April, 1862, and in October moved
to an island in Lake Erie. This island later housed Confederate POW's.

Barclay Coppoc once went to Salem to see a traveling panorama of
Harpers Ferry.

Lewis Leary's widow became the grandmother of the poet,
Langston Hughes.

Dangerfield Newby's wife and children were sold down river
to Louisiana.

The two books on Old Brown's nightstand were the Bible
and a biography of Cromwell.

It was Cromwell who first said, *Kill 'em all, let God sort 'em out.*

Old Brown published journal articles about sheep.
He won a World Medal in Brussels.

Barclay Coppoc died in 1861 when the train he was riding on plunged through a burning bridge into the Platte River. The fire had been lit by Confederate irregulars.

Old Brown said a prayer each morning asking God
for the liberation of the oppressed all over the world.

Old Brown ate dinner with Emerson and Thoreau.

In February, 1953, a great crowd of Chinese at Peking greeted
the arriving Dr. W.E.B. Dubois. They sang "John Brown's Body,"
with its chorus of "Glory, Glory hallelujah, his soul goes marching on."

Harriet Tubman was sick the day of the raid.

Henry Higginson became literary executor of Emily Dickinson.

As he passed around broadswords by camp light on the bank of
Potawatamie Creek, Old Brown said to his boys, *Do something witchy.*

Edwin Coppoc drew a bead on Robert E. Lee, but the hostage Jesse W. Graham, who tells this story, begged him not to shoot. And he didn't. Of such gossamer is history made.

Cook blamed Douglass for the raid's failure, claiming Douglass had been assigned to bring a body of men to the Kennedy house where arms were stored, but had failed due to cowardice.

Cook wrote poetry the day he was hanged.

The Coppock letter in the New York Tribune was denied by Coppock. It is alleged to be written by Cook and signed with Coppock's name.

Douglass wrote from Canada: *Wholly, grievously, and most unaccountably wrong is Mr. Cook, when he asserts that I promised to be present in person at the Harpers Ferry insurrection. . . . I have never made a promise so rash and wild as this. The taking of Harpers Ferry was a measure never encouraged by my word or by my vote, at any time or place. . . . I desire to be quite emphatic here, for of all guilty men, he is the guiltiest who lures his fellow-men to an undertaking of this sort, under promise of assistance which he afterwards fails to render.*

Some enterprising fellow painted "John Brown's Fort"
above the engine-house's triple arches, and hawkers sold
bogus pikes to tourists riding the B & O.

The fort was deconstructed brick by brick and shipped to the
Columbia Exposition in Chicago. Only no one was interested
in paying ten cents to see it.

In the Colorado Super-Max, Timothy McVeigh, Ramzi Yusef, and
Ted Kosinski talked at length about Old Brown, whom each claimed
as his political progenitor.

On his way to the scaffold, as he descended the steps of the jail,
Old Brown spotted in the crowd a black woman holding her child.
Brown bent over and kissed the child.

The scaffold was bought for $900 and sold to relic hunters.

In Easton, Pennslyvania, a man selling a biography of Old Brown
received a dozen lashes and was forced to leave town.

In Virginia, a New Englander thought to be an Abolitionist was hung
from a tree until nearly dead, then revived and hung again, four times.
Once each for Old Brown, Coppick, Cook and Stevens.

Old Brown fired the first shot of the Civil War.
Old Brown freed the slaves.

THEY LAID OLD BROWN

They laid out Old Brown in the parlor,
bony as Che' on the table. Executed,
like Dillinger at the Biograph, like
Jesse James standing on Mr. Howard's chair,
like the Younger brothers, peppered rabbits
stretched in their Northfield coffins.
Like Bonnie & Clyde shivering in the front seat
of a Texas summer.

As if that proves anything.
Where are the missing morgue photos
of Pretty Boy Floyd, after all?
Why so many death masks cast?
See that scrape, that hole,
that mole, it can't be him.

He has eluded Death's algebra,
its silent figuring:
trajectory, entry and exit,
magic bullets.

You know, they charged admission to look
at Old Brown's body, propped it up
and dropped nickels into his open mouth.
Bits of Old Brown's beard were
sold in early vending machines.

Only that wasn't Old Brown wounded
in the armory and hung in Charleston.
He escaped to Bolivia with Butch & Sundance,
was bombed in Spain with the Abraham Lincoln Brigade.
Always the blurry one in the photo, he appears
in the background of Sandinista billboards.

KILLING KING COTTON

He brought down King Cotton,
threw down his house around him,
cut off his head and staked it at the crossroad.
He broke the Gin, cracked its backbone
and sucked the marrow.
He has greased the wheels,
bent the rails into hairpins.
He would carry the war to Africa,
for the Alleghenies are God's bower.
Lawrence went up like an Ohio Blue-Tip.
The Murrah Building went up like an Ohio Blue-Tip.
The Towers went up like Ohio Blue-Tips.
He was an Angel of Light, an Angel of Fire,
an Agent of the New England Emigrant Aid Company,
purveyor of Kansas Furniture and Chicago Typewriters.
He lived on the Moonfire Ranch,
was wrong on the goose, and this wasn't Kansas anymore.
For he crossed the River Jordan at Wellsville.
For he made of the gallows a cross.
For he broke the teeth of apologists.
Because the eyes of the world were upon him.
Because the whole world was watching.
For he lived like a toad under the harrow.
For he looked like a meat axe.
So he parked the yellow Ryder at the Dreamland Motel.
So he killed The Good Death.
So he offered up three sons
upon the bitter rock of Slavery.

HUNGRY GHOST

I have scoured the Greensboro newscast
for footage of Old Brown.
It is an eight millimeter haunting.
He is a hungry ghost,
pencil-necked and pinhole mouthed.
Truth turns to ashes in his mouth.

Each side points their guns at the other.
Each reach like drowning men,
reach like children with cap guns,
like God reaching to Adam.
It's an American home movie,
corny as Gunsmoke. In it
dead men fall funny, drop
like puppets cut from strings.

Haymarket, Homestead, Blair Mountain.
These are water lanterns slipping downriver.
Grant Park, OK City, Blanket Hill.
These are water lanterns slipping downriver.

He stood in the gauntlet at Homestead,
ball-peen hammer nicely balanced in his hand,
from interstate overpasses dropped cement blocks
into the laps of passing scabs.
The blocks came through the windshield,
startling as the hand of God.
He lobbed hand grenades at the National Guard.
He fired the first shot on Blanket Hill.
In Chicago he lit a flare, shouting:

> *The Whole World is Watching!*
> *The Whole World is Watching!*
> *The Whole World is Watching!*

SUNSHINE YELLOW RYDER

The yellow Ryder, a bright square of diesel-powered
sunshine packed with ammonium nitrate, pulled out
of the Dreamland Motel. Old Brown rode shotgun.
At the red light he lit the fuse with a Cuban cigar.
Smoke filled the cab as they waited for the change.

When it came, Old Brown opened the door and
stepped down like a Teamster, or The Marlboro Man.
He leaned back into the window, said,
Do something witchy, then disappeared
down the sidewalk.

He is the unidentified accomplice,
missing piece of every assassination's puzzle.
His townhouse is smaller than Ted Kozinski's cabin.
He builds bombs in the basement. He walks on eggshells.

The State Police pulled over Old Brown's Mitsubishi
just outside Chambersburg. He drove without a license and
his vanity plates read GDS HAMR. He wore a t-shirt that said:
The Tree of Liberty Must Be Watered With the Blood of Patriots.
Sic Semper Tyrannis!, he shouted at the startled trooper.

In one pocket was *The Turner Diaries,*
in the other, *The Confession of Nat Turner.*
In his vest was Mao's Little Red Book.
At home, on his nightstand,
were a black Bible and a biography of Cromwell.

KEELHAULED IN GOD'S WAKE

Truth hath no confines.

Truth is Justice's drunken sister.
She jaywalks, spits on the sidewalk,
burns books in the courtyard,
pulls tongues from the root.
She jigs and reels on the monster's grave.

Truth is electrodes and genitalia.
A truth in hand is worth two in the bush.
Truth splits hairs, is a hostile witness.
She should be strapped to a board,
or dunked in a barrel.
It only seems like drowning.

Truth sees both sides of a story,
slips her handcuffs, escapes the bunker.
She is plain, unvarnished,
and hides in plain sight.
Truth is gray as a bagful of God,
stranger than fiction.
Truth is booted out of choppers over the Atlantic,
buried alive in Pentagon file cabinets.
Sometimes she is hard to take.

Truth shares a bed with Consequence,
says, *Show me*, believes it when she sees it.
Truth won't drink the Kool-Aid,
gets all the beads at Mardi Gras.
Truth be told, but never is.
She is whole and there is nothing else.

I STOOD WITNESS

I stood in an ocean of wheat, awash to the waist.
I stood witness to God's tornadic eye,
watched His great grey finger as it
traced the divine word across the landscape.

His great head swiveled this way, then that,
His face all eye and featureless as an egg.
His horizon was infinite.

Great Ginny, He sorted them out,
sorted cotton from seed.
He was piston-elbowed,
and howled like a locomotive.
He had to burn the village to save it,
had to make a clean sweep of it.

He is like straw driven through a 2x4,
the straw that breaks a camel's back,
conqueror of hearts and cities.

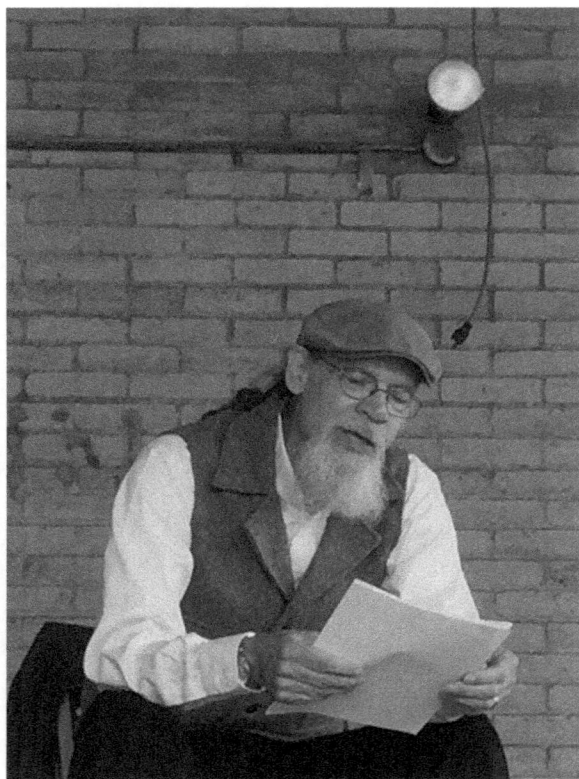

About the Author

Craig Paulenich is a Professor of English at Kent State University, a founder and professor of the Northeast Ohio Master of Fine Arts Program. He is the author of two books of poetry, *Drift of the Hunt* (Nobodaddies Press, 2006), and *Blood Will Tell* (BlazeVOX [books], 2009), and editor (with Kent Johnson) of *Beneath a Single Moon: Buddhism and Contemporary American Poetry* (Shambhala Press, 1991), a landmark anthology of poems and essays from forty-five American Buddhist poets. He has been three times nominated for a Pushcart Prize, by *Nobodaddies* (1994), *Seems* (2002), and the *Kelsey Review* (2009). His poems have appeared in *The Georgia Review*, the *South Carolina Review*, *Kansas Quarterly*, and the *Southern Poetry Review*, and many others. Professor Paulenich holds an M.F.A. in Poetry from the University of Pittsburgh, and a Ph.D. in English from Bowling Green State University. He and his wife Karla live on a farm in Lisbon, Ohio.

BOOKS BY BOTTOM DOG PRESS
HARMONY SERIES

Taking a Walk in My Animal Hat, by Charlene Fix, 90 pgs, $16
Earnest Occupations, by Richard Hague, 200 pgs, $18
Pieces: A Composite Novel, by Mary Ann McGuigan, 250 pgs, $18
Crows in the Jukebox: Poems, by Mike James, 106 pgs, $16
Portrait of the Artist as a Bingo Worker: A Memoir, by Lori Jakiela, 216 pgs, $18
The Thick of Thin: A Memoir, by Larry Smith, 238 pgs, $18
Cold Air Return: A Novel, by Patrick Lawrence O'Keeffe, 390 pgs, $20
Flesh and Stones: A Memoir, by Jan Shoemaker, 176 pgs, $18
Waiting to Begin: A Memoir, by Patricia O'Donnell, 166 pgs, $18
And Waking: Poems, by Kevin Casey, 80 pgs, $16
Both Shoes Off: Poems, by Jeanne Bryner, 112 pgs, $16
Abandoned Homeland: Poems, by Jeff Gundy, 96 pgs, $16
Stolen Child: A Novel, by Suzanne Kelly, 338 pgs, $18
The Canary: A Novel, by Michael Loyd Gray, 196 pgs, $18
On the Flyleaf: Poems, by Herbert Woodward Martin, 106 pgs, $16
The Harmonist at Nightfall: Poems of Indiana, by Shari Wagner, 114 pgs, $16
Painting Bridges: A Novel, by Patricia Averbach, 234 pgs, $18
Ariadne & Other Poems, by Ingrid Swanberg, 120 pgs, $16
The Search for the Reason Why: New and Selected Poems, by Tom Kryss,
192 pgs, $16
Kenneth Patchen: Rebel Poet in America, by Larry Smith,
Revised 2nd Edition, 326 pgs, Cloth $28
Selected Correspondence of Kenneth Patchen,
Edited with introduction by Allen Frost, Paper $18/ Cloth $28
Awash with Roses: Collected Love Poems of Kenneth Patchen,
Eds. Laura Smith and Larry Smith with introduction by Larry Smith, 200 pgs, $16
Breathing the West: Great Basin Poems, by Liane Ellison Norman, 96 pgs, $16
Maggot: A Novel, by Robert Flanagan, 262 pgs, $18
American Poet: A Novel, by Jeff Vande Zande, 200 pgs, $18
The Way-Back Room: Memoir of a Detroit Childhood, by Mary Minock, 216 pgs, $18

BOTTOM DOG PRESS, INC.

P.O. BOX 425 /HURON, OHIO 44839
HTTP://SMITHDOCS.NET